Voices of Freedom

The Emancipation Proclamation

Karen Price Hossell

LIBRARY

Chicago, Illinois

© 2006 Heinemann Library
a division of Reed Elsevier, Inc.
Chicago, Illinois
Customer Service: 888-454-2279
Visit our website at www.heinemannlibrary.com

Printed in China by WKT Company Limited
10 09 08 07 06
10 9 8 7 6 5 4 3 2 1

Library of Congress Cataloging-in-Publication Data:
   Price Hossell, Karen, 1957-
 The Emancipation Proclamation / Karen Price Hossell.
    p. cm. -- (Voices of freedom)
 Includes bibliographical references (p.   ) and index.
 ISBN 1-4034-6813-3 (hc) -- ISBN 1-4034-6818-4 (pb)
 1. United States. President (1861-1865 : Lincoln). Emancipation Proclamation--Juvenile literature. 2. Slaves--Emancipation--United States--Juvenile literature. 3. Lincoln, Abraham, 1809-1865--Juvenile literature. I. Title. II. Series.
 E453.P87 2005
 973.7'14--dc22

                          2005006263

Acknowledgments
The publisher would like to thank the following for permission to reproduce photographs:
Corbis pp. 4 (James L Amos), 7 (Nathan Benn), 9, 14, 16, 21, 22, 23, 24, 29, 30, 31 (Bettmann), 32, 33, 35 (Bettmann), 36, 38 (Bettmann), 39, 40, 41 (Bettmann), 42 (Bettmann), 43 (Bettmann), 44 (Reuters/Frank Polich); Getty Images p. 5 (Photodisc); Heinemann Library p. 6 (Jill Birschbach); Library of Congress pp. title, 8, 11, 15, 18, 20, 25, 26, 27, 28, 37; National Archives & Records Administration p. 34; Photo Edit p. 45 (Bob Daemmrich); The Granger Collection, New York pp. 10, 12, 13.

Cover image of a slave reproduced with permission of Corbis.

Some words are shown in bold, **like this**. You can find out what they mean by looking in the glossary.

Contents

Recording Important Events

One way to know about what happened in the past is by reading documents written by people who were witnesses to history. Some of these documents are letters about events written by people who were there when the events occurred. Other kinds of important historical documents might be **memoirs** written by people who were in a war or by presidents or other leaders after they left office. Records of history that provide a firsthand account of an event are called primary sources. When several primary sources of the same event are gathered together, they can provide us with a more complete story of the event.

Primary sources also include drafts of speeches and official papers that were carefully planned. The people involved in the planning and writing of these documents were often careful to make sure the words in the documents expressed their exact thoughts. Other kinds of primary sources include videos or sound recordings. They can be of events such as the first man on the moon or the events of the attack on the World Trade Center on September 11, 2001.

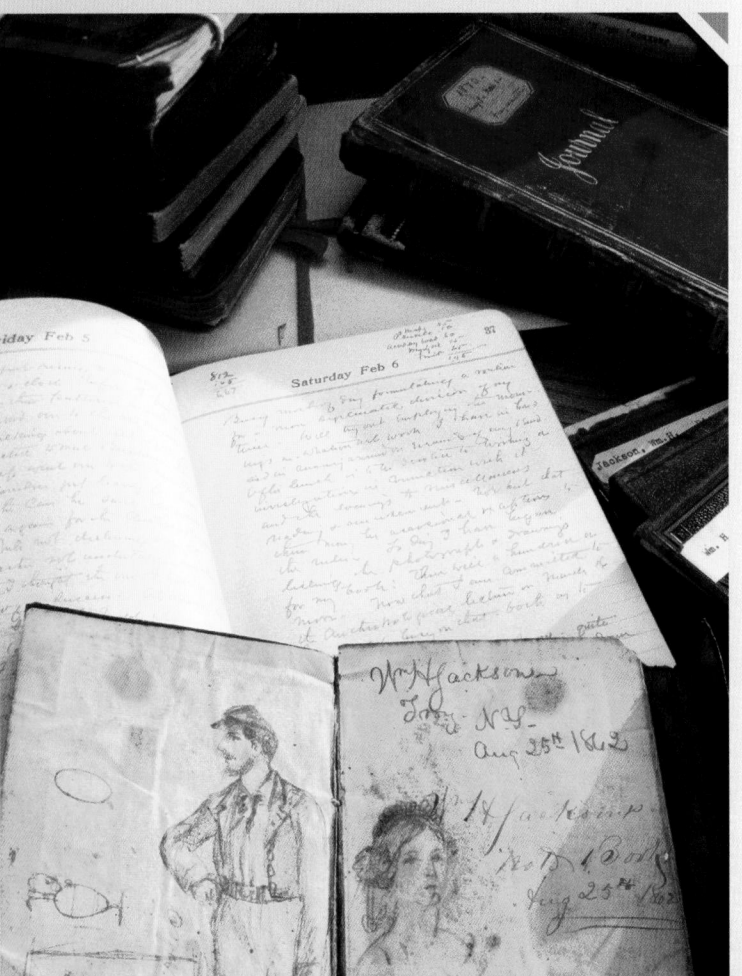

Most of the time when someone creates a primary sources he or she is not planning on creating a source for historians to use. Instead, the person is probably simply writing in a diary, or recording an important event.

Primary sources are important because they tell us what happened in the words of people who lived through a time or event. Most written documents contain some of a writer's opinion. As time passes, opinions of an event often change. For example, a person writing about the Civil War today would probably have a different opinion of the events than a person who was writing as the fighting was going on.

Knowing what people thought about an event at the time can help us to better understand the event.

Secondary sources

Another category of sources are those written by people who have studied primary sources. These are secondary sources. Scholars study these and write their own books and articles based on their research. When you write a research paper for school you are creating a secondary source. However, if in the future someone wants to study how students wrote research papers in the 21st Century, your paper could become a primary source.

Secondary sources are usually based on primary sources. Both are valuable to scholars and researchers.

Storing and Preserving Historical Documents

Protecting the primary and secondary sources that make up our historical records is so important that those records are kept in buildings devoted to that purpose. The records are kept in buildings where people can enjoy them and study them. In the United States two of the best-known places are the National Archives and Records Administration, or NARA, and the Library of Congress. An archive is a place where documents are stored.

The Library of Congress

The Library of Congress is in Washington, D.C. It is a federal institution and also the largest library in the world. Its collection is available to members of Congress as well as to the rest of the American public. The Library of Congress holds about 120 million items, including maps, books, and photographs.

The National Archives and Records Administration (NARA)

The original documents in the NARA collection provide a history of the United States government. NARA houses paper documents and films, photographs, posters, sound and video recordings, and other types of government records. These documents also tell the story of American settlement, industry, and farming. In fact, documents and other **artifacts** detailing almost every aspect of American history can be found in the NARA collection.

The Library of Congress is the country's oldest government run cultural institution. It has about 530 miles of bookshelves.

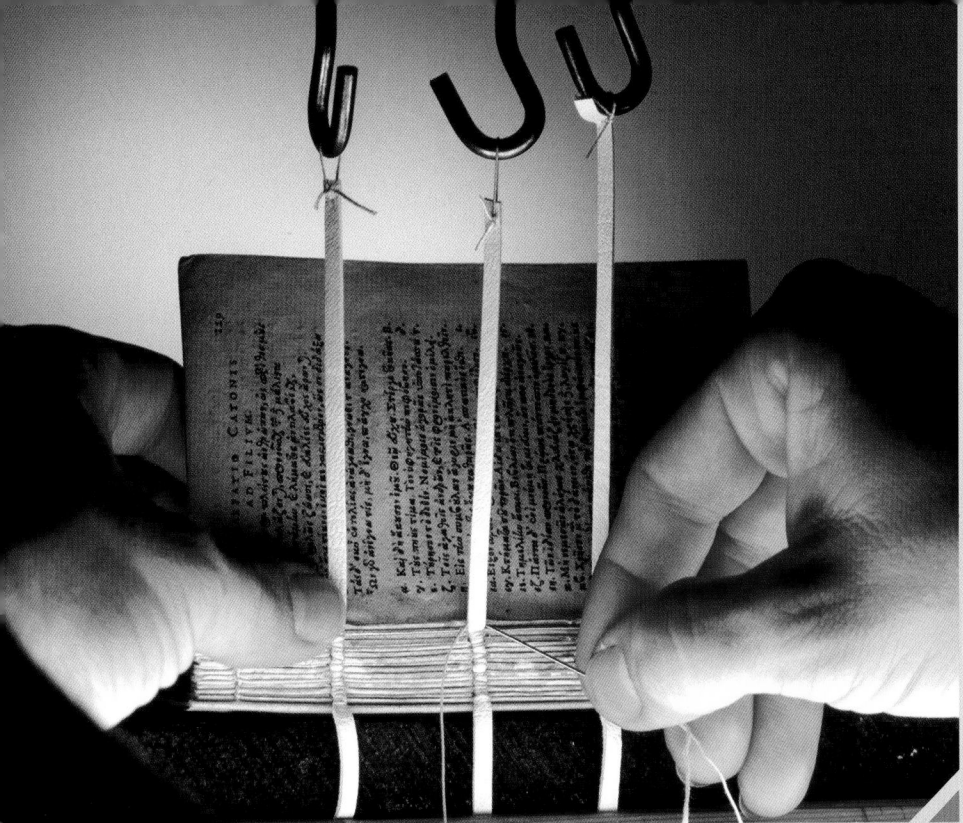

A sixteenth century technique is being used to restore this book with a needle and thread.

Among the documents stored in the NARA is a group of documents called the Charters of Freedom. They include the United States Constitution, the Bill of Rights, and the Declaration of Independence. These historical records are on display in the public area of the NARA.

In 1998 **conservators** at the NARA became concerned about the condition of the Charters of Freedom, so they closed the public exhibit. Then they carefully removed each document from its bulletproof and fireproof glass case and closely examined it for damage. They found that in some cases the ink had faded from the parchment, so they had to repair the document using special techniques.

Special storage facilities

Other paper records in the NARA are stored in specially designed boxes. Because paper gets darker over time, documents can become hard to read. The documents are kept in special boxes that keep the paper from darkening. The boxes are stored in fireproof, locked stacks. The temperature and humidity, or wetness, in NARA storage areas are carefully controlled, because heat and humidity can damage documents.

Conservators also know how to protect tape recordings, videotapes, photographs, and other kinds of artifacts. In the future, people will be able to look at these documents just as we study the Declaration of Independence and other historical records.

What Is the Emancipation Proclamation?

On January 1, 1863, people all over the United States waited to see if President Lincoln's promise to free the slaves would be fulfilled. As the hours ticked by, many wondered if the president had changed his mind. In the South, the struggle to survive continued, with slaves working in the fields or in the **plantation** homes of their owners. Northerners who had fought against slavery for years waited for the news in churches and auditoriums, singing hymns and listening to anti-slavery speeches.

This draft of the Emancipation Proclamation is in Lincoln's handwriting.

News traveled by telegraph in those days. People who lived out in the countryside who were not near a telegraph office often learned about events days, even weeks after they happened. But it wasn't long before most Americans heard the news that President Lincoln had signed the document that declared the slaves living in slave states were free. That document was called the Emancipation Proclamation. The four pages that make up the proclamation are among the most important pieces of paper in American history.

The Union and the Confederacy

In the years before President Lincoln signed the Emancipation Proclamation, the United States had divided into two sections. One was the Union, which was made up of states in the North. The other was the Confederacy, which was made up of states in the South. For a long time, the differences between these two areas of the country had been clear. In the North, most people lived in large cities such as New York, Philadelphia, and Boston. Many others lived in small towns, and some lived on small farms. There were some large farms in the North, too, but not nearly as many as in the South.

Much of the land in the South was owned by people who had been wealthy in England. They had been given large plots of land for doing favors for the English king. Many of them moved to America, built large homes, and grew crops on the land. These large farms were called plantations. For plantation owners to make money from their crops, they had to hire people to work for them. But it was difficult for them to find people to work for low wages. In time, they came up with a way to find labor for free.

Slavery had existed in America since 1619. The first slaves were indentured servants, which meant they worked for someone for a specific period of time—usually seven years—and then were freed. But as plantations grew, more workers were needed. Slave trading companies formed. They made a business of buying and selling people. They sailed ships to Africa, kidnapped the African people, chained them together, and forced them onto cramped, filthy ships. They sailed the Africans to America and sold them as slaves. Plantation owners and their managers bought slaves at markets in cities such as Charleston, South Carolina, and New Orleans, Louisiana.

The Africans were brought to plantations and forced to live in terrible conditions with barely enough food. As slaves they were forced to work at least six days a week, often for fourteen or more hours a day.

This picture from 1860 shows slaves disembarking in Key West, Florida.

Slavery in the United States

Many Southerners realized that without slaves, their plantations would fail. People in both the North and the South understood that much of America's **economic** strength depended on the goods that plantations **exported**, such as tobacco, rice, and cotton. So for a long time, few people spoke out against slavery. They knew it was wrong, but most Americans believed it was the best system they could come up with for getting the work done.

This engraving from the mid 1800s shows a typical Southern plantation.

When the American colonies declared themselves to be independent from Great Britain and became the United States of America, some political leaders wanted slavery to be outlawed because it was not fair. They hoped a law against owning slaves would be included in the United States Constitution. But most leaders, including George Washington, knew that Southern states would never agree to a Constitution that included such a law. These leaders believed that it was important to have a strong, united nation, not one divided by the issue of slavery, so slavery continued.

In 1808 Congress passed a law making the slave trade illegal—in other words, people could no longer be removed from Africa and brought to the United States and sold. But this law did not apply to the slaves who were already living in the United States. Children born to slaves were also slaves, so slavery continued to exist.

The Dred Scott Case

Dred Scott was a slave who was born in Virginia. When he was about thirty, his master died and Scott was sold to a military surgeon named Dr. John Emerson. Scott traveled with Dr. Emerson as he moved from one military post to another. Some of the states they lived in were free **territories** such as Illinois and Wisconsin. Because slavery was not legal in those states, Scott wondered whether he was still legally a slave when he lived there, but he did not ask for his freedom. After Dr. Emerson died, though, a lawyer helped Scott file a case against Emerson's widow saying that because he had lived in territories that did not have slaves, he should be free. The case went to the United States **Supreme Court** in 1857. All Americans were interested in the outcome of the case, because it could change slavery forever.

But the Chief Justice of the Supreme Court, Roger B. Taney, supported slavery. He and the other justices decided that slaves were still slaves even when they lived in free territories. They also said that black people, whether they were slaves or not, could never become United States citizens. Additionally, they decided that the laws that banned slavery in certain United States territories were **unconstitutional**. Scott died only a few months after this decision, still a slave.

The court's decision was important to many Americans because it divided the nation. The decision made most Southerners happy and many Northerners angry.

The Life of an American Slave

The kind of life a slave had depended on several things. One was the type of plantation the slave worked on. Slaves on cotton plantations did hours of backbreaking work in the hot sun. They picked cotton from sunup to sundown, bending over and pulling the fluffy cotton bolls from the prickly plants. Slaves on tobacco plantations did not fare much better. As the soil used to grow tobacco grew old and infertile, new fields had to be cleared. Slaves cut down trees, ground down stumps, and removed rocks from fields, then planted the tobacco and picked it when it was ready. On most rice plantations, life was a little easier because the task system was used. Each slave was assigned a task, and when he or she completed it, the day's work done.

Other kinds of work

Slaves also worked in their master's homes as housekeepers, cooks, nannies, and butlers. Some men were employed as carriage drivers, others as carpenters who helped build homes and furniture. Slaves were also hired out to do work for other people in the community. But the only things slaves ever received from their masters was food, clothing, and shelter—not money. The child of a slave was automatically a slave, and children as young as six worked in the fields.

These workers are picking cotton on a Southern Plantation. Even though the Civil War was over by the time this photograph was taken, working conditions had not changed much for African Americans. The photograph is black and white, but it has been painted over with oil paint.

This painting depicts an idealized view of the life of house slaves. Young slave children sometimes played with their master's children until they were old enough to work.

A Slave's Story

Henry Bibb, a slave in Shelby County, Kentucky wrote this account of his early life as a slave. Bibb escaped from slavery as an adult and lectured about its evils.

I was taken away from my mother, and hired out to labor for various persons, eight or ten years in succession; and all my wages were expended for the education of Harriet White, my playmate. It was then my sorrows and sufferings commenced [began]. It was then I first commenced seeing and feeling that I was a wretched slave, compelled to work under the lash [whip] without wages, and often without clothes to enough to hide my nakedness. I have often worked without half enough to eat, both late and early, by day and night. I have often laid my wearied limbs down at night to rest upon a dirt floor, or a bench, without any covering at all, because I had no where to rest my wearied body, after having worked hard all the day. I have also been compelled in early life, to go at the bidding of a tyrant [bully], through all kinds of weather, hot or cold, wet or dry, and without shoes frequently, until the month of December, with my bare feet on the cold frosty ground, cracked open and bleeding as I walked.

The Anti-Slavery Movement

Some Americans were so against slavery that they worked to put an end to it. At first this work was called the anti-slavery movement. Later, the people who actively worked to end slavery were called **abolitionists**, and the movement was called abolition.

Some abolitionists were against slavery for religious reasons. They believed that all people were created to be equal and to live peacefully together, and that no one should be owned by another. For them slavery was one of the most evil things ever created by man.

Some people saw John Brown as a fighter for justice and freedom, others saw him as a terrorist willing to murder in the name of a cause.

John Brown

Perhaps the most well-known abolitionist was John Brown. He went as far as to murder people who supported slavery. Brown's most famous act occurred in 1859, when, with 21 other abolitionists, he took over a United States-owned **arsenal** at Harpers Ferry, Virginia. Brown hoped to use the weapons there in his fight against slavery. Instead, General Robert E. Lee, head of the Confederate Army, overpowered Brown and his men. For his act of **treason**, Brown was hanged on December 2, 1859. Many abolitionists looked at Brown as a hero, but few used tactics as violent as his.

Harriet Tubman and the Underground Railroad

Some abolitionists were former slaves. One of them was Harriet Tubman. Harriet was born in about 1820—because she was a slave, there is no official record of her birth —in Dorchester County, Maryland. When she was only about seven years old, she was hired out to do work. Because she was so young, she sometimes did not do a very good job. Once she was whipped for not obeying her master, and she ran away and hid in a hog pen for four days, eating the food that was supposed to go to the hogs.

Harriet discovered that she was best at working in the fields. She liked being outside, where she could think her own thoughts, and she was known to have been as strong as many men. But when her master died, things changed. She found out that her brothers and sisters were going to be sold to different plantations and that she might never see them again. One day, she met a woman who told her that if she was at a certain place at a certain time, someone would help her. Harriet wanted her freedom, and she wanted to help her brothers and sisters gain their freedom, too. She showed up at the place the woman mentioned, and an abolitionist helped her get to another place. A person there helped her continue her journey. On one leg of her journey, Harriet hid under a sack in the back of a wagon. This chain of events went on until Harriet found herself in Ohio, a state that did not allow slavery. Once in Ohio, Harriet realized she was free.

The people who helped Harriet were in a group called the Underground Railroad. They helped slaves escape, then provided food and shelter for them, hiding and protecting them as they traveled north to freedom. Harriet was so grateful for these people that she became a part of the Underground Railroad, eventually helping more than 300 slaves to freedom. Eventually, she ended up in Philadelphia, where she worked cleaning houses.

Harriet Tubman was rescued by the Underground Railroad, and then used it to help others.

Slaves Who Rebelled

It was not unusual for slaves to run away like Harriet Tubman did. Often, these slaves were hunted down and returned to their masters. Instead of running away, some slaves rebelled in other ways. They became so angry by the fact that they were slaves that their anger turned to violence. One violent slave rebellion was led by Nat Turner.

Turner was born on a small plantation in Southampton County, Virginia. From a young age, his intelligence impressed those who knew him. Because he was a slave, Turner was unable to use his intelligence to help himself or his family.

This illustration shows Nat Turner being approached by a slave hunter in the woods.

Once Turner ran away and hid in the woods for a month. While he was hiding, he believed that God spoke to him, telling him to return to his master. There, God said, he would discover what he was born to do. Turner returned and began preaching to other slaves. He was such a great speaker that his master allowed him to travel from plantation to plantation, preaching to the slaves there. But while Turner was allowed to travel, he was still a slave who was owned by his master. If he tried to run away, he could be hunted and captured, even killed.

Turner begins the rebellion

Turner began to believe that he saw visions from God and that signs told him to stage a rebellion. He and some other slaves he trusted began to hide weapons, such as heavy tools and axes, in the woods. On August 20, 1831, they met in the woods, picked up the weapons, and went to the home of Turner's master, Joseph Travis. They beat and killed Travis, his wife, and other family members, including a baby.

The gang then went on to kill more people in the area—all together, they murdered 57 people. But then they came up against a **militia** that was searching for them. The two sides engaged in a gun battle, and the slaves fled. Turner ran back to the Travis plantation, dug a hole in the ground, gathered food, and hid there for weeks. Eventually, he was found, put on trial, found guilty, and hanged.

Living in fear

Uprisings such as the one Turner and his followers carried out put fear into the hearts of many southerners. They were afraid for their lives, and on many plantations this fear gave slaves a certain amount of control. On other plantations, slave masters became stricter with their slaves. For example, they no longer allowed their slaves to visit slaves living on other plantations.

States also enacted laws to keep slaves in check. People in northern states often thought that these laws were wrong. But the southern states said they had the right to make any laws they wanted. They even threatened to **secede**, or leave the United States, if Congress tried to stop them from making these laws.

17

The Nation Divides

In the mid-1800s, the southern states threatened to leave the Union if Congress passed laws that southerners didn't like. To keep the southern states happy, Congress passed a series of laws, known as the Compromise of 1850. Some of these laws, such as outlawing slavery in Washington, D.C, were passed to make the North happy. Some of the laws, such as giving Texas $10 million to give up territory in New Mexico, were passed to please the South. The two sides agreed in order to keep the nation together. One of the laws included admitting California into the Union as a free, or nonslave, state.

The Compromise worked because it kept the Union together for a while. But the division between the North and South continued. By 1859 Americans in the South feared slave uprisings and were angered by the ideas of **abolitionists**. They were also angry that the North did not seem interested in enforcing the Fugitive Slave Act of 1850. This law allowed Southern slave owners to hire people to find and arrest slaves who had run away to the North and return them to the **plantation**.

Although he was president at the time, James Buchanan did nothing to stop the southern states from seceding.

Lincoln is elected president

In 1860 it was time to elect a new president. By that time, some in the South wanted to leave the United States and create their own slave-holding nation. When Abraham Lincoln won the election for president, Southerners thought life as they knew it was over. They knew Lincoln was against slavery and believed he would make it illegal. Without slaves, southern plantations would not be able to produce crops and sell them. Plantation owners would lose money, possibly even their land. Even Southerners who did not own plantations agreed that **secession** might be necessary.

On December 20, 1860, South Carolina took action and declared itself out of the Union. Lincoln would not become president officially until his **inauguration** in January of 1861, and the president at the time, James Buchanan, did nothing about South Carolina. Before Lincoln's inauguration, six more states seceded—Alabama, Florida, Georgia, Louisiana, Mississippi, and Texas. Buchanan still did nothing. What United States leaders had feared had now come true. The Union was officially divided.

This map shows the Confederacy and the Union at the beginning of the Civil War.

The Fugitive Slave Act of 1850

President Millard Fillmore signed the Fugitive Slave Act into law in 1850. The act appointed slave commissioners to hunt down runaway slaves, arrest them, and return them to their masters. But while they saw the act as a way to protect their property, many Southerners became angry when it seemed as if Northerners were not willing to enforce the act. Some of them believed this so strongly that they used it as one of the reasons they no longer wanted to be part of the United States.

Abraham Lincoln

Who was this man that so many in the South hated? Abraham Lincoln was born in a log cabin in Hardin County, Kentucky, on February 12, 1809, and went on to become one of the most well-known presidents the United States has ever known. As a boy Lincoln loved to hunt and fish, but he also loved to read. Because he lived so far out in the wilderness, he only spent about a year in regular school—most of what he learned as a young man was what his stepmother taught him or what he taught himself by reading books.

This is rare portrait of a young Abraham Lincoln.

As a young man Lincoln had several jobs, but eventually he became a lawyer. With a friend, he opened a law practice in 1837 in Springfield, Illinois. Throughout his life he considered Springfield his hometown.

Before he began practicing law, Lincoln was elected to the state **legislature**. People liked his simple style and believed that he was truly interested in their concerns. In Springfield, Lincoln spent most of his evenings in the back of the local general store. With his friends, he would sit around a fireplace and discuss politics and current events. It was here, historians say, that Lincoln first developed his **debating** and speaking skills.

This shows President Lincoln's home in Springfield, Illinois. Today, the home is open to visitors, and a new museum has been constructed nearby.

Debating

These skills were further polished when Lincoln ran for United States Senate against Stephen Douglas in 1858. Lincoln challenged Douglas to a series of debates, and the two men traveled to seven Illinois cities that year. Large crowds gathered to hear the men debate slavery. Lincoln spoke against slavery, and Douglas supported it.

Lincoln was elected senator, and when it was time to pick a candidate for president in 1860, he became the choice of the newly formed Republican party.

Lincoln on Slavery

Lincoln did not like slavery, but he did not actively work to end it until he became president. He wrote to his friend Joshua Speed in 1855 that:

I confess that I hate to see the poor creatures [slaves] hunted down, and caught, and carried back to their stripes, and unrewarded toils; but I bite my lip and keep quiet. In 1841 you and I had together a tedious low-water trip, on a Steam Boat from Louisville to St. Louis. You may remember, as I well do, that ... there were, on board, ten or a dozen slaves, shackled together with irons. That sight was a continual torment to me; and I see something like it every time I touch the Ohio or any other slave-border.

In another letter he wrote in 1859, just before he was elected president, Lincoln wrote, "he who would be no slave, must consent to have no slave. Those who deny freedom to others, deserve it not for themselves; and, under a just God, can not long retain [keep] it."

The Civil War Begins

In 1860 the United States had 34 states. The states in the South that **seceded** from the Union formed the Confederacy, and named Jefferson Davis as their president. The rest of the states were still the United States, but were commonly called the Union, and Lincoln was their president.

Jefferson Davis became the President of the Confederacy.

Fort Sumter

The Union had two forts in the South. One was Fort Pickens in Florida's Pensacola Bay. The other was Fort Sumter in Charleston Harbor, just outside Charleston, South Carolina. The Confederate Army did not like that a Union-controlled fort was sitting right outside Charleston. On April 10, 1861, the Confederates decided to order the Union troops in Fort Sumter to leave, and threatened to bomb the fort if they stayed. The troops remained, and the Confederate Army's boats surrounded the fort and bombarded it. Finally, Major Anderson, the head officer at the fort, surrendered to Confederate troops on April 13.

With this battle, the Civil War had begun. It was to become the only war fought on U.S. soil since the birth of the nation, and the only war in which Americans fought Americans. By the end of the war, more than 600,000 people had died. That is more than all of the other wars the United States has fought in combined.

The Confederacy grows

In the spring of 1861, four more states seceded from the Union—Virginia, North Carolina, Arkansas, and Tennessee. Now the Confederacy had eleven states, the Union twenty-three. The Confederacy set up its capital in Richmond, Virginia.

After these states seceded, the Union began to worry that the states that bordered the Confederacy would secede, as well. The Confederates worked to persuade these states—Delaware, Missouri, Kentucky, and Maryland—to join them. But the border states remained in the Union throughout the war.

Know It!

While most of the state of Virginia agreed to secede in the spring of 1861, those who lived in the western part of the state refused and declared that they were still in the Union. In June of 1863, this section of Virginia officially became the state of West Virginia.

This photograph shows the 8th New York State **Militia** at camp.

The Preliminary Emancipation Proclamation

In April 1862 Congress abolished slavery in Washington, D.C., and in United States **territories**. In July 1862 Congress passed the Second **Confiscation** Act, which said that any slaves who escaped from the South and made it inside Union lines were free. In addition, any slaves who worked for the Union Army would be declared free. Lincoln realized that weakening the institution of slavery would weaken the Confederacy, because their **economy** and way of life depended on it.

Writing the Proclamation

With Union leaders, Lincoln began to discuss the idea of **emancipating** the slaves. He liked to go to the War Department to await telegrams that gave news of the outcomes of battles. One of the men in the telegraph room said that in July 1862, Lincoln asked him for some writing paper. Lincoln took up a pen to write the first draft of what turned out to be the Preliminary Emancipation Proclamation. He came back to the telegraph office several times to continue to work on the paper, telling people he could concentrate better away from the White House.

Once he finished the document, Lincoln wanted to immediately announce it to the nation. But his advisors told him to wait until after the Union had won a major battle.

This African-American union troop was based near Washington, D.C.

The Union Army, however, was not doing so well. The Confederacy won most of the important early battles. Finally, however, the Union won a decisive victory on September 17, 1862, at the Battle of Antietam in Maryland. More than 5,000 soldiers from both armies died in this battle. More than 20,000 were injured. After he heard about the Union victory, Lincoln ordered Union General McClellan to continue fighting the Confederates until their army was destroyed. However, McClellan hesitated, and the Confederate Army escaped to the south.

The announcement

Still, the victory strengthened the North's determination to continue to fight to repair the Union. On September 22, Lincoln announced the Preliminary Emancipation Proclamation, saying that he intended to free all slaves in the Confederacy by January 1, 1863, unless Confederate states rejoined the Union. Lincoln hated slavery and believed it was wrong. But he stated in the Preliminary Emancipation Proclamation that his reason for writing it was not simply because slavery was wrong but to bring the Union back together. Lincoln knew that some freed slaves living in the North would join the Union Army to fight against the Confederacy. He also knew that the **abolition** of slavery would weaken the Confederacy. Finally, he realized that the issue of slavery was actually at the heart of **secession** and was becoming one of the central issues of the war.

This is a page from Lincoln's final draft of the Emancipation Proclamation.

Recolonization

In the Preliminary Emancipation Proclamation, Lincoln included the idea of recolonization. This meant that he wanted to send the freed slaves back to Africa to live. Lincoln would do this only with the consent of the slaves. He would not force anyone to go to Africa, but he believed that freed slaves might be happier to be returned to the land from where their ancestors were kidnapped.

The Emancipation Proclamation

The states in the Confederacy had no intention of rejoining the Union to prevent their slaves from being freed. They had formed their own separate nation, and they no longer considered Lincoln to be their president. So even if he ordered that the slaves were free, the Confederacy would not recognize that order.

Lincoln had hoped that the Preliminary Emancipation Proclamation would serve as a warning to the Confederacy. They had been given three months to rejoin the Union—if they did not, their slaves would be freed. But the Confederate states continued to rebel.

On December 29, 1862, Lincoln met with his advisors, where he read the Emancipation Proclamation aloud. Then he asked if anyone had suggestions for ways to improve it. After making a few changes, Lincoln decided the Proclamation was ready to be announced to the public.

African-American men, women, and children are shown gathered around waiting for the Emancipation Proclamation to be read.

War powers

When the day came for the Emancipation Proclamation to be signed, Americans, both Union and Confederate, waited anxiously. Would Lincoln keep his promise? Soon, they discovered that he would. To make sure the proclamation had as much power as it could, he signed it not as president of the United States but as commander-in-chief of the United States military. As president, he could not legally declare a proclamation such as this one. First, the proclamation would have to go through **Congress** and be voted on. But as commander-in-chief, Lincoln had what were called "war powers," which meant he could make certain decisions during wars without going to Congress. The Emancipation was such an order.

Decorated copies of the Emancipation Proclamation were popular souvenirs.

The Words of the Emancipation Proclamation

In the opening statement of the Emancipation Proclamation, Lincoln writes that in any state that is in rebellion against the United States—that is, any state in the Confederacy—the slaves will be free. His government will recognize all slaves from these states as free, and will not try to stop them from trying to gain their freedom.

Illustrator Thomas Nast created this hopeful version of life after Emancipation.

WHEREAS, on the twenty-second day of September, in the year of our Lord one thousand eight hundred and sixty-two [1862], a Proclamation was issued by the President of the United States, containing, among other things, the following, to wit:

That on the first day of January, in the year of our Lord one thousand eight hundred and sixty-three [1863], all persons held as slaves within any State or designated [named] part of a State, the people whereof shall then be in rebellion against the United States, shall be then, thenceforward, and forever, free; and the Executive government of the United States, including the military and naval authority thereof, will recognize and maintain the freedom of any such persons, and will do no act or acts to repress such persons, or any of them, in any efforts they may make for their actual freedom.

Here, the proclamation says that any states that send representations to **Congress** by January 1, 1863, will be considered not in rebellion. The Emancipation Proclamation would then not apply to those states.

That the Executive will, on the first day of January aforesaid, by proclamation, designate the States and parts of States, if any, in which the people thereof, respectively, shall then be in rebellion against the United States; and the fact that any State, or the people thereof, shall on that day be in good faith represented in the Congress of the United States, by members chosen thereto at elections wherein a majority of the qualified voters of such States shall have participated, shall, in the absence of strong countervailing testimony, be deemed conclusive evidence that such tate, and the people thereof, are not then in rebellion against the United States.

"Forever Impossible"

On January 12, 1863, Jefferson Davis is quoted as saying that the Emancipation Proclamation meant that "a restoration of the Union has been rendered forever impossible." The Confederacy he led would not recognize such a document, so unless they were defeated, they would continue to act as if the proclamation had never happened.

A slave being released from his bonds. The Emancipation Proclamation did not actually free all slaves, just those living in the Confederacy.

More about the Words of the Proclamation

Now, therefore, I, ABRAHAM LINCOLN, President of the United States, by virtue of the power in me vested as Commander-in-chief of the Army and Navy of the United States, in time of actual armed rebellion against the authority and government of the United States, and as a fit and necessary war measure for suppressing [ending] said rebellion, do, on this first day of January, in the year of our Lord one thousand eight hundred and sixty-three, and in accordance with my purpose so to do, publicly proclaimed for the full period of one hundred days from the day first above mentioned, order and designate as the States and parts of States wherein the people thereof, respectively, are this day in rebellion against the United States, the following, to wit...

Lincoln declares here that as commander-in-chief, he is issuing the proclamation as a war measure. He is doing it, he writes, to suppress—or try to put an end to—the rebellion of the Confederate states.

President Lincoln, as Commander in Chief, is shown meeting with Union troops.

But the proclamation was limited in what it provided. The slaves that it freed were in the eleven states of the Confederacy, which was led by Jefferson Davis, not Lincoln, so the United States government did not have control there. Lincoln names those states that were in rebellion, but lists the counties in those states that did not go along with the rebellion. The end of slavery would only be ensured if the Union won the war.

And by virtue of the power and for the purpose aforesaid, I do order and declare that all persons held as slaves within said designated States and parts of States are and henceforward shall be free; and that the Executive government of the United States, including the military and naval authorities thereof, will recognize and maintain the freedom of said persons.

And I hereby enjoin upon the people so declared to be free to abstain [stop] from all violence, unless in necessary self-defense; and I recommend to them that, in all cases when allowed, they labor faithfully for reasonable wages.

And I further declare and make known that such persons, of suitable condition, will be received into the armed service of the United States to garrison forts, positions, stations, and other places, and to man vessels of all sorts in said service.

And upon this act, sincerely believed to be an act of justice warranted by the Constitution upon military necessity, I invoke the considerate judgement of mankind and the gracious favor of Almighty God.

In this passage, Lincoln declares all slaves in the rebellious states to be free. He tells the freed slaves not to react by behaving violently toward those who had enslaved them. He also encourages them to find paid labor. Lincoln goes on to tell the slaves that they will be accepted into the United States Army if they qualify, and that he believes the Emancipation Proclamation to be a just act that is supported by the Constitution and necessary because of the war.

This painting shows Abraham Lincoln reading the Emancipation Proclamation to his presidential cabinet members.

The Nation and the World React

Even before the Emancipation Proclamation became official, people rejoiced. When the Preliminary Emancipation Proclamation was issued in September 1862, former slave Frederick Douglass wrote:

"We shout for joy that we live to recall this righteous moment ... long enslaved millions, whose cries have so vexed the air and sky, suffer on a few days in sorrow, the hour of your deliverance draws nigh! ... lift up your voices with joy and thanksgiving for with freedom toe the slave will come peace and safety to your country."

In the months between the Preliminary Emancipation Proclamation and January 1, 1863, many Americans continued to celebrate. Even some people in the South were glad to see slavery end, but most Southerners felt it was a dark day in their history.

Waiting and praying

On the night before President Lincoln was to sign the Emancipation Proclamation— New Year's Eve, 1862—African Americans in Northern cities such as Boston put lit candles in their windows. Many of them went to church, where they sang and prayed in anticipation of the joy they hoped the New Year would bring. Whites visited many of the churches as well, and joined in the singing and praying.

Frederick Douglass was a former slave who worked for the freedom of others.

This engraving shows African Americans celebrating the end of slavery in their state. The Emancipation Proclamation did not end slavery in the border states.

On New Year's Day, the Boston Music Hall filled with **abolitionists** who listened to a concert of classical music and sang hymns. They sat inside the auditorium all day, waiting for a telegram to bring them the news. Just before midnight the telegram arrived, and everyone cheered, cried, and hugged. Similar scenes took place in Washington, D.C., where as soon as the news was delivered, members of the Israel Bethel Church, according to their pastor, the Reverend Harry Turner, "raised a shouting cheer that was almost deafening." In Norfolk, Virginia, slaves who had walked off **plantations** marched on the city to the home of the military governor on January 2. The cities of Washington, D.C., Pittsburgh, Buffalo, and New York greeted the news with 100-gun salutes.

In Europe people also celebrated. However, some political leaders in England had hoped to support the Confederacy in the near future, possibly joining with them to defeat the Union and bring the United States under British rule again. They were not happy about the proclamation, but most people felt like the crowd of people at a meeting in Manchester, England. Upon hearing the Proclamation, they cheered for the end of slavery and booed whenever the South was mentioned.

Know It!

Frederick Douglass was born a slave in Maryland, but escaped in 1838 when he was twenty. He went on to become an abolitionist, speaking all over the United States against slavery.

The Thirteenth Amendment

Because the Emancipation Proclamation did not pass through Congress, it was not actually a law. However, it did allow Union troops to protect freed slaves during the Civil War, and when slaves crossed into Union territory, they were automatically free. Slavery was not actually illegal in the United States, though, until Congress passed the Thirteenth **Amendment**.

The thirteenth amendment of the Constitution outlaws slavery.

The Thirteenth Amendment was passed by the United States Senate on April 8, 1864. It went to the House of Representatives, but failed to be passed there even though all of the representatives voting were from the north. President Lincoln worked to persuade members of the House to pass the bill, and they finally did on January 31, 1865. On December 6, 1865, enough states had **ratified** the amendment for it to become law.

The amendment says that:

> **Amendment XIII [13]**
> **Section 1.** *Neither slavery nor involuntary servitude, except as a punishment for crime whereof the party shall have been duly convicted, shall exist within the United States, or any place subject to their jurisdiction.*
>
> **Section 2.** *Congress shall have power to enforce this article by appropriate legislation.*

How Amendments Are Made

Amendments are passed by Congress—which is made up of the Senate and the House of Representatives—then sent to state **legislatures**. The legislatures vote whether to ratify the amendments. Three-fourths of the states must vote for ratification for amendments to be included in the Constitution.

"Involuntary servitude" refers to forcing any person to work as a slave or servant without their consent, except as punishment for a crime, which usually refers to imprisonment. With the addition of this amendment in the United States Constitution, slavery was illegal in the United States, and slaves were finally and completely free. Now the nation had to recover from a long and devastating war.

Amendments change the U.S. Constitution. Sometimes an amendment overrules a Supreme Court decisions, such as the 13th amendment overruled the Dred Scott case. Here, President Nixon is shown signing the 26th amendment to the Constitution. The 26th amendment gives 18-year-olds the right to vote.

A Slave's Story

Henry Adams was a slave who testified before Congress in 1880 about what happened on the day he found out about the Emancipation Proclamation. This is part of what he said:

The white men read a paper to all of us colored people telling us that we were free and could go where we pleased and work for who we pleased. The man I belonged to told me it was best to stay with him. He said, 'The bad white men was [sic] mad with the Negroes because they were free and they would kill you all for fun.' He said, stay where we are living and we could get protection from our old masters. I told him I thought that every man, when he was free, could have his rights and protect themselves. He said, 'The colored people could never protect themselves among the white people. So you had all better say with the white people who raised you and make contracts with them to work by the year for one-fifth of all you make. And next year you can get one-third, and the next you maybe work for one half you make. We have contracts for you all to sign ... I told him I would not sign anything ... but he said again, 'Sign this contract so I can take it to the Yankees and have it recorded.' All who lived on the place was about sixty, young and old.

After the War

The Civil War took a terrible toll on the United States. More than half a million people died in its battles. The nation was torn apart. Homes and businesses were burned by troops, and families, crops, and livestock were destroyed.

Abraham Lincoln was another victim of the war. He never saw the Thirteenth Amendment become law. On April 9, 1865, the war ended with a Union victory. On April 14, just five days after the Confederacy surrendered to the Union and ended the war, Lincoln was watching a play in Washington, D.C. when he was shot in the head by John Wilkes Booth. He died the next morning. Booth had supported the South during the war. He hated Lincoln for freeing the slaves and for suggesting in a speech on April 11 that it might be a good idea to give some blacks the right to vote.

Lincoln's death was a blow to the nation. He had led them through one of the most difficult periods in American history, and in the end his goal of preserving the Union had been met. Many wished he could have led them through the next difficult period, Reconstruction.

This is the last photograph Lincoln posed for. He is shown with his son, Tad.

Reconstruction

After the Civil War, the nation had to find a way to rebuild what had been destroyed. Most of the destruction had occurred in the South, because most of the fighting had occurred there. The destruction affected physical property such as homes, businesses, and crops. But is also had an impact on the way Americans thought about their nation and one another. The secession of the Southern states had caused a great wound to the nation that would take years to heal.

Congress passed Reconstruction Acts in 1867 that established laws and procedures for rebuilding the nation. The acts provided a way for the former Confederate states to ease back into the Union.

In March of 1865, Congress established the Freedman's Bureau, which protected the interests of former slaves. The bureau helped freed slaves find jobs and built schools and hospitals for them. In April of 1866, Congress attempted to pass a Civil Rights Bill that would protect freed slaves against Southern Black Codes, which were laws in the South that discriminated against them. But Andrew Johnson, who became president after Lincoln died, **vetoed** the bill.

The First Years of Freedom

Soon after the war ended, **Congress** passed two important **amendments**. The Fourteenth Amendment, passed in 1868, made citizens of all African Americans born in the United States. It also made state laws that discriminated against blacks illegal. The Fifteenth Amendment, passed in 1870, gave African American men the right to vote.

This is a typical school for blacks during Reconstruction.

The power to vote

Now that African American men could vote, they chose John W. Menard to represent them in government. In 1868 John W. Menard was elected to the United States House of Representatives. His Louisiana voting district was fifty percent black. When the loser challenged Menard, however, Congress decided that neither man would serve in Congress.

Two years later, a black man was admitted in the United States Senate when Hiram Revels of Mississippi was voted in. During Reconstruction, twenty African Americans from the South were elected to the United States House of Representatives, and two were elected to the Senate.

The Ku Klux Klan

Hundreds of African Americans—many of whom were former slaves—held public office in the South, a reflection of the high percentage of blacks who lived in those states. Many white Southerners felt powerless when those who had only recently been considered underneath them now represented or governed them.

Their frustration led to the founding of an organization called the Ku Klux Klan in Tennessee in 1866. The Klan wanted to stop blacks from voting. They also attacked—and often killed—former slaves who had successful businesses.

This image of the Ku Klux Klan is from 1872.

The Struggle Continues

Besides the Freedman's Bureau, which was intended to last for only one year, **Congress** passed other Acts designed to help newly freed slaves. The Enforcement Codes were passed in 1870 and 1871. They were designed to protect African Americans' right to vote, to hold office, to serve on juries, and to be protected by laws. If the state government refused to enforce these codes, the **federal** government was allowed to step in and see that they were followed.

In 1875, Congress passed a Civil Rights Act that guaranteed that all races had equal access and enjoyment of public facilities, which included libraries. But in 1883 the United States **Supreme Court** declared the act to be unconstitutional. Congress, the court said, had no power to tell individuals not to discriminate against others.

Violence and terror in the South

These civil rights laws were passed in part as a reaction to the violence and terror the Klan was spreading throughout the South. Often, Klansmen would take the law into their own hands and lynch black men they thought broke the law without putting them on trial. Many times, Klan members were also members of law enforcement, so blacks had little chance of fair treatment. Members of the Ku Klux Klan and other racist groups also terrorized and killed Republicans because members of that party supported civil rights for blacks. In Vicksburg, Mississippi, for example, they killed seventy-five Republicans.

Freedman's bureaus were set up to help recently freed, sick, and old slaves. Here, people stand in line for aid.

Sharecropping

Once slavery ended, fields and crops still had to be tended, and freed slaves needed work. Slaves and their former masters worked out a system called sharecropping. This meant that the landowner provided the land, mules to pull the plows, and seed. Blacks provided the work and got a share of the crops. They sold their share and kept the money.

This system worked for a while, but as time passed, landowners took advantage of sharecroppers. Many found it almost impossible to save enough money to buy their own land, and the sharecropping system continued in some areas well into the twentieth century.

In 1938 these sharecroppers were living in a former slave shack.

Exodusters

After the war, federal troops stayed in the South to enforce laws, especially those made by Congress to protect freed slaves. During Reconstruction, some freed slaves remained on plantations and worked for pay, or became sharecroppers and grew crops, or moved North to work at low-paying jobs. After the troops left the South in 1877 and violence and racism began to grow, a large number of slaves left the South. Many went North, but about 50,000 went West to Kansas. They were helped by a former slave named Benjamin "Pap" Singleton, who had encouraged blacks to go where they would be completely free and where the land was fertile for farming. They were called "Exodusters" because their movement west was a great exodus from the South.

Jim Crow Laws

In the 1870s, Democrats began to take over state governments in the South. In an attempt to keep the races separate and because they feared that blacks were gaining too much power, Democratic leaders in Southern states passed a series of laws designed to separate the races. The laws forbade people from associating with those of another race. The most common Jim Crow laws kept people of different races from marrying and forced races to be separate in public places.

For example, in Texas, African Americans had separate libraries, with black librarians. In Georgia, there were laws against burying blacks in cemeteries that were set aside for whites. In Florida and other states, the blacks and whites were taught in separate schools. In most states, whites and blacks could not be served in the same dining room in a restaurant. In Alabama, for example, diners had to sit in separate rooms, or one room had to have a divider that was at least seven feet high. In Louisiana, a law said that circuses had to provide two separate ticket sellers, and if they were outdoors, they had to be at least 25 feet apart. Blacks and whites could not even go into the circus tent in the same entrance; circus owners had to make sure there were at least two separate entrances, one for blacks, and one for whites.

Segregation was common in the South.

Plessy vs. Ferguson

In 1892 this system of separating the races was challenged by Homer Plessy. He boarded a train in Louisiana and sat in a car designated for whites, even though he was part black. Plessy refused to move and was arrested. The case went all the way to the **Supreme Court**, which decided that the separation of races did not violate the Fourteenth Amendment of the United States Constitution. The court found that since both races had equal facilities, the law that separated them was fair. This concept is sometimes called "separate but equal."

Brown v. Board of Education

These laws of separation remained in place for many years. Then, in 1954, another case was brought before the Supreme Court called *Brown v. Board of Education*. This case again tested the "separate but equal" concept. Linda Brown was a young African American girl who lived near a school for whites. Because of "separate but equal" laws, however, she had to travel to a different school. The National Association for the Advancement of Colored People (NAACP) took her case to court, claiming that racial separation, or **segregation**, went against the United States Constitution. The Court agreed and decided that separating people by the color of their skin means they are not being treated equally. This decision marked the end of segregation in the United States. The Civil Rights Movements of the 1950s and 1960s that followed this decision helped African Americans make great gains, one hundred years after slaves were emancipated.

Know It!

Jim Crow laws were named after a character in minstrel shows. In a minstrel show, white entertainers put on a "black face," meaning that they put make-up on to look as if they were African American. These white men portrayed blacks in a negative way.

In 1954 the Supreme Court outlawed school segregation.

The Legacy of the Emancipation Proclamation

The **Emancipation** Proclamation is one of the most important documents in American history. It righted a wrong that had persisted for more than two hundred years. It also changed the way of life for millions of Americans. Where before it had been legal for people to own slaves, in most parts of the United States it became illegal. Planters who had a large, cheap work force now had to pay laborers to work for them. Slaves suddenly had the freedom to do whatever they wanted, but few had the skills and education to find work outside of farm or **plantation** labor.

Besides the freedom of slaves, one of the greatest legacies of the Emancipation Proclamation is the creation of schools and colleges to educate African Americans. These include Howard University in Washington, D.C.; Stillman College in Tuscaloosa, Alabama; and Wilberforce and Central State Universities in Ohio.

Barack Obama of Illinois was elected to the U.S. Senate in 2004. He was only the third African American to become a senator since Reconstruction ended.

This cavalry unit is celebrating Juneteenth day, a holiday that celebrates the end of slavery.

The proclamation and the Thirteenth **Amendment** that followed it made slaves free, but African Americans had an uphill climb to live as freely as other Americans. They faced discrimination in the form of Jim Crow and other laws and terrorist groups such as the Ku Klux Klan. It took a long time to right the wrongs of slavery—many would argue that the journey is continuing, and that the United States still has a way to go before African Americans are treated with the same respect and sense of equality as white Americans.

The Importance of the Document

Recently, the NARA and a few other organizations got together and asked the American people which documents they considered to be the most important in American history. The Emancipation Proclamation was voted the fifth most influential document in the United States.

The original copy of the Emancipation Proclamation is in the National Archives. It is five pages long and written in Lincoln's hand. The document was originally tied with red and blue ribbons that were attached to the document with a wax seal. Today, the seal is almost gone, but most of the ribbons are intact.

For a long time, the document was bound with other important papers in a large volume and kept by the United States Department of State. In 1936, the department transferred the Emancipation Proclamation to the National Archives. It is in fragile condition and is rarely on public display.

Glossary

abolitionist person who worked to end slavery

amendment change. In the Constitution, amendments are formal changes voted on by states.

arsenal place where weapons are stored

artifact object made and used by someone in the past

confiscate taking something that is not yours because a law says you may do so

congress formal meeting of delegates for discussion and usually action on some question; lawmaking body of the United States government

conservator person who is responsible for the care, restoration, and repair of documents and other historical artifacts

debate formal discussion in which two sides of an issue are represented

deteriorate become damaged in quality, condition, or value

economy system of buying and selling; how a nation makes money

emancipation the act of freeing something

export to take goods from one country to another, usually to sell them

foolscap writing paper

immigrant person who moves to another country to live

inauguration ceremony during which the United States president is officially sworn in

legislature group of elected individuals who make laws for those who elect them

memoir firsthand written record of something that happened in the past

militia ordinary citizens with some military training banded together in a military unit

minstrel shows popular in the 1800s and 1900s in which white people blackened their faces and told jokes and performed songs and dances associated with African Americans

plantation large farm, usually in the South, often with slaves

proclamation formal announcement made public

ratify vote to officially approve or accept

secede to leave or separate from something

secession the act of removing from-during the Civil War, southern states seceded, declaring they were no longer part of the United States

segregation forced separation of people of different races

Supreme Court highest court in the United States; some cases that deal with specific issues of law go to the Supreme Court to be discussed. The decision of the Supreme Court almost always stands.

territory part of the United States that is not a state. Many present states were first territories.

treason when a person commits a crime against their nation or government

unconstitutional going against the United States Constitution, which is the document of written law upon which the United States government is based

veto refusal to approve

More Books to Read

January, Brendan. *Cornerstones of Freedom: The Emancipation Proclamation.* Danbury, CT: Children's Press, 1998.

Martin, Michael. *Let Freedom Ring-The Civil War: The Emancipation Proclamation: Hope and Freedom for the Slaves*. Minneapolis: Bridgestone Books, 2002.

Places to Visit

The National Civil War Museum
One Lincoln Circle at Resevoir Park
Harrisburg, PA 17105
(866) 258-4729
www.nationalcivilwarmuseum.org

Index